DATE			

Native Americans

Chumash

Barbara A. Gray-Kanatiiosh

ABDO Publishing Company

visit us at
www.abdopub.com

Published by ABDO Publishing Company, 4940 Viking Drive, Suite 622, Edina, Minnesota 55435. Copyright © 2004 by Abdo Consulting Group, Inc. International copyrights reserved in all countries. No part of this book may be reproduced in any form without written permission from the publisher.

Printed in the United States.

Cover Photo: Corbis
Interior Photos: Corbis pp. 4, 28, 29, 30
Illustrations: David Kanietakeron Fadden pp. 7, 9, 11, 13, 15, 17, 19, 21, 23, 25, 27
Editors: Kate A. Conley, Jennifer R. Krueger, Kristin Van Cleaf
Art Direction & Maps: Neil Klinepier

Library of Congress Cataloging-in-Publication Data

Gray-Kanatiiosh, Barbara A., 1963-
    Chumash / Barbara A. Gray-Kanatiiosh.
       p. cm. -- (Native Americans)
    Summary: An introduction to the history, social structure, customs, and present life of the Chumash Indians. Includes bibliographical references and index.
    ISBN 1-57765-933-3
    1. Chumash Indians--History--Juvenile literature. 2. Chumash Indians--Social life and customs--Juvenile literature. [1. Chumash Indians. 2. Indians of North America--California.] I. Title. II. Native Americans (Edina, Minn.)

E99.C815G72 2003
979.4004'9757--dc21

2003044374

About the Author: Barbara A. Gray-Kanatiiosh, JD

Barbara Gray-Kanatiiosh, JD, Ph.D. ABD, is an Akwesasne Mohawk. She resides at the Mohawk Nation and is of the Wolf Clan. She has a Juris Doctorate from Arizona State University, where she was one of the first recipients of ASU's special certificate in Indian Law. Barbara's Ph.D. is in Justice Studies at ASU. She is currently working on her dissertation, which concerns the impacts of environmental injustice on indigenous culture. Barbara works hard to educate children about Native Americans through her writing and Web site, where children may ask questions and receive a written response about the Haudenosaunee culture. The Web site is: www.peace4turtleisland.org

About the Illustrator: David Kanietakeron Fadden

David Kanietakeron Fadden is a member of the Akwesasne Mohawk Wolf Clan. His work has appeared in publications such as *Akwesasne Notes*, *Indian Time*, and the *Northeast Indian Quarterly*. Examples of his work have also appeared in various publications of the Six Nations Indian Museum in Onchiota, NY. His work has also appeared in "How the West Was Lost: Always the Enemy," produced by Gannett Production, which appeared on the Discovery Channel. David's work has been exhibited in Albany, NY; the Lake Placid Center for the Arts; Centre Strathearn in Montreal, Quebec; North Country Community College in Saranac Lake, NY; Paul Smith's College in Paul Smiths, NY; and at the Unison Arts & Learning Center in New Paltz, NY.

Contents

Where They Lived

Chumash (CHOO-mash) homelands were located in what is now California. Their territory included parts of present-day southern California and the Channel Islands. Their neighbors included the Yokut, Salinan, and Gabrielino.

The Chumash lived along the coast, on islands, and inland. The Coastal Chumash lived along the shores of the Pacific Ocean. Their land had beaches, dunes, and **estuaries**. Shrubs, willow trees, and **tule** (TOO-lee) grew on their land.

The Island Chumash homelands were on islands in the Pacific Ocean. They lived on the Santa Cruz, Santa Rosa, San Miguel, and Anacapa Islands. These islands were home to many plants and animals.

The Inland Chumash homelands had mountains, rivers, and stands of oak trees. The territory was bordered by the

Chumash cave paintings

San Joaquin (san-wah-KEEN) Valley and the western coast of California. This territory included Mount Pinos, near present-day Santa Barbara. The Chumash considered Mount Pinos sacred.

The Chumash spoke about eight related languages. These languages were from the Hokan language family.

Chumash Homelands

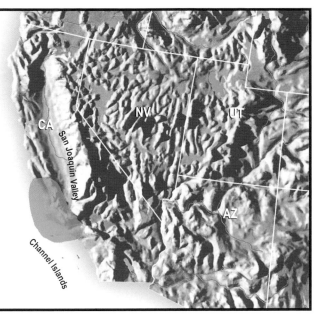

5

Society

Chumash society was **tiered**. At the top of the society were the medicine people and astrologers. Astrologers helped guide the Chumash by carefully watching and charting the stars.

Chiefs called *wot* ranked just below the medicine people and astrologers. A man or a woman could inherit the title of chief. A chief had many duties. These duties included feeding the poor, protecting the people, and arranging hunting and gathering trips. Ceremonial leaders and messengers helped the chiefs with these duties.

The skilled artisans were below the chiefs. The artisans made items such as beads, which were used for trade and decoration. Below the skilled artisans were the laborers. The poor class was at the bottom.

Opposite page: A Chumash astrologer charts the stars in the sky.

Food

The Chumash hunted, fished, and gathered their food. Inland, they used bows and arrows to hunt mule deer, bears, and mountain lions. The Chumash also hunted rabbits, quails, ducks, and songbirds. They caught these animals in traps, snares, and nets. They used a long, curved throwing stick that looked like a boomerang to hunt rabbits.

Along the shore and on the islands, the Chumash hunted sea mammals. These animals included seals, otters, pilot whales, and porpoises. The Chumash used **harpoons** for this type of hunting.

The men fished using basket traps. The traps were designed to let the fish swim into the trap's wide, open end. It led to a narrow, closed end that stopped the fish from escaping. The Chumash also used a hook and line to fish. They made hooks from **abalone** shell and lines from twisted plant fibers.

When fishing in the ocean, the men caught sharks, halibut, and bonitos. Inland, they fished for trout. The Chumash also harvested shellfish such as mussels, clams, and **abalone**.

The Chumash women gathered berries, cherries, wild plants, seeds, cattails, pine nuts, and acorns. Acorns were a staple food for the Chumash. They roasted the acorns and ground them into flour. Then, they made the flour into mush and cakes. The Chumash stored their food in large **granaries** woven from willow.

A Chumash man hunts a rabbit with a throwing stick.

Homes

There were about 100 villages throughout Chumash territory. The settlements consisted of extended families that lived in homes called 'ap (AHP). The homes were shaped like domes and covered in thatch. The Chumash built these homes near the water.

The frame of a Chumash home was made with willow poles. To build a frame, the Chumash put the ends of sapling willow poles in the ground. They bent the poles at the top to meet in the center, forming a dome.

Next, the Chumash tied on cross poles with **cordage** made from milkweed fibers. This made the frame sturdy. Sometimes, the Chumash used whalebone to make the frame even stronger.

The Chumash covered their homes with thatch mats. They made the mats from **tule**, bulrush, or cattail stalks. They tied the mats onto the frame, leaving a hole at the top to let smoke out and light in. They could close the hole with a cover made of animal skin.

Chumash homes

As many as 40 to 50 people lived in one home. Around the inside of the home, each person had his or her own private area. They slept on platforms. Inside the home there was also a fire pit. The fire provided warmth and a place to cook.

Outside each home was a sweathouse built over a deep pit. The Chumash used a ladder to get in and out of the pit. They placed hot rocks inside. They poured water over the rocks, causing steam to fill the sweathouse.

Clothing

In warm weather, the Chumash did not wear much clothing. When they did wear clothing, it was made of woven bird feathers, animal skins, and plant fibers. In the winter, the Chumash wore capes made from animal hides. They also wore capes made of woven rabbit skins and plant fibers.

Men wore nets around their waist. They used the nets like pockets to carry water jugs and other items. The nets were made of **cordage** woven from milkweed fibers and bird **down**. Woodpecker, magpie, gull, and hawk feathers were attached to the netting.

Chumash men also wore ceremonial **kilts**. The kilts were strands of cordage that hung down from the waist. The Chumash tied whole bird feathers to the ends of these cords.

Chumash women wore cordage skirts. They also wore dresses. Women made their dresses by sewing together patches of rabbit or bird skins. They decorated their clothing with shells.

The Chumash tied their hair on the top of their heads with a string. Men wore a forehead band of orange-colored **flicker** feathers.

Both men and women often wore sandals and painted their bodies. To make the paint, they mixed milkweed sap with colored minerals. Each village had its own design.

Chumash clothing

Crafts

The Chumash had many artistic skills. Chumash men practiced the craft of making beads from **olivella** shell. Making shell beads took a lot of time and patience. These beads were valuable and used as money.

The Chumash were also excellent basket makers. Some baskets were for everyday use. Others were made as gifts or for use in ceremonies. The Chumash decorated their baskets with **geometric** designs using dyes made from plants.

The Chumash made three types of baskets. Coil baskets could hold liquids. These baskets were woven with bulrush and willow. Then the Chumash put hot rocks and crushed asphalt into the baskets. As the hot rocks melted the asphalt, the baskets became waterproof.

Twine baskets could be used for gathering and storing seeds, meal, and water. The Chumash used twine to make seed beater baskets. Seed beater baskets looked like a bird's nest on a short twig. The seed beater knocked seeds off grasses and into a gathering basket.

Coarsely woven baskets had many uses, too. Some people used these baskets as strainers. The Chumash also used these baskets as traps. They used the traps to catch fish.

A Chumash basket maker

Family

The men, women, and elders in Chumash families had different responsibilities. Women gathered food and cooked. Men made tools and other items. And, the elders helped raise the family.

Women used digging sticks to unearth **edible** roots and bulbs. Soap plant bulbs were a favorite of the Chumash. They roasted and ate the green bulbs. But, the bulbs could also be used as soap!

Chumash women also worked with steatite, a type of stone. They cooked in steatite ollas, which are containers used for cooking and storage. They baked on flat cooking stones. The men of a Chumash family also worked with steatite. They carved beads, bowls, and charms from steatite.

Men were also responsible for making plank canoes from redwood. They drilled and lashed redwood planks together. Then they sealed the seams and drill holes with asphalt. The asphalt made the plank canoes waterproof. If they got a splinter while working, the Chumash would remove it with clamshell tweezers.

Chumash elders also had a special role in their families. They helped raise the children. For example, the Chumash elders would often teach the children about sacred rock paintings.

Chumash men tend to their redwood plank canoe.

Children

The Chumash carried their babies on basketry **cradleboards**. The Chumash wove their cradleboards from **tule** or willow.

As the children grew, they learned by watching and helping the adults. For example, Chumash girls learned how to make baskets. They learned how to prepare rabbit skins and weave them into blankets. They also learned how to strip milkweed plants for **cordage**.

Chumash boys learned how to hunt and fish. They learned how to craft the tools they needed, such as fishing traps. They also made **sinew**-backed bows and bird-**down** arrows.

Chumash children often watched as artisans made beads and bird-bone hairpins. The children also had time to run, swim, and play games. For example, they played a game of dice with walnut shells filled with asphalt. They determined their points by how the dice landed.

A young
Chumash boy
uses a basket
trap to catch fish.

19

Myths

The Chumash have a myth about how their people were created. A long time ago, the earth was very quiet. Earth Mother, Hutash, decided to make humans. Humans could fill the earth with beautiful sounds.

Hutash created the Chumash from magic seeds and placed them on an island. The island was located in the Pacific Ocean near present-day Santa Barbara. Sky Snake, who was Hutash's husband, sent down a bolt of lightning. This brought fire to the Chumash.

Soon, the Island Chumash became very noisy. Hutash was getting a headache from all the noise. She decided the time had come to move some of the people. She created a rainbow bridge. The bridge reached from the island to the mainland.

Hutash said, "It is time for some of you to cross the bridge. The mainland has everything you will need to live in peace."

Some Chumash crossed the bridge. They found the coast and the inland to be beautiful and full of wonderful foods.

But along the way, some of the people fell off the bridge. Hutash did not want her people to drown. So, she turned the fallen people into dolphins.

The Island Chumash travel on a rainbow to the mainland.

War

The Chumash were a peaceful and friendly people. They usually got along with their neighboring tribes. So, they did not go to war often.

It was the chief's job to arrange the use of hunting, fishing, and gathering territory in other communities. If the other community did not grant permission, a war between the two groups would break out.

When the Chumash went to war, they used bows and arrows. For close combat, they fought with knives made from flint or shell. Men often carried small flint knives in their hair.

The Chumash were organized in battle. First, they sent a messenger to their enemy. The messenger arranged the time when the battle would happen.

At the set time, the Chumash met the other group. They threw feathers into the air and shouted war cries. One side shot a series of arrows at the other side. Then, the other side shot the same number of arrows. After each side shot its arrows, the conflict ended.

A Chumash man goes into battle with his bow and arrows.

Contact with Europeans

The Chumash are believed to have been the first major California tribe to meet Europeans. A brief meeting took place with Portuguese explorer Juan Rodríguez Cabrillo. In 1542, he left Mexico and discovered California. He eventually sailed into what is now Santa Barbara Channel.

In 1602, Spanish explorer Sebastián Vizcaíno met the Chumash. He arrived and anchored off the coast on the feast day of Saint Barbara. So, his landing spot was named Santa Barbara.

The Chumash were friendly to the Europeans. In the 1700s, the Spaniards, with help from some of the Chumash, built Roman Catholic **missions** on Chumash lands.

Opposite page: Juan Rodríguez Cabrillo meets the Chumash.

Many Chumash became part of the **missionary** system. But, learning the ways of the missions caused many Chumash to lose their languages and traditions. Many Chumash also died from sicknesses the Europeans had brought with them. The Chumash had no **immunity** to illnesses such as **smallpox** or the common cold.

Chumash Leaders

The Chumash had many leaders over the years. Some tried to prevent the Spaniards from converting the people to Christianity. Others thought conversion was good.

One Chumash leader who converted to Christianity was Chief Pedro Yanonali. He helped the Spaniards when they were setting up **missions** in the area. Over time, other Chumash also converted to Christianity. But today, many Chumash leaders believe the Spanish missions put the Chumash way of life in danger.

Today, leaders are working hard to protect the Chumash **culture**. Mati Waiya, or Little Hawk, is one such person. He is a Chumash ceremonial leader. He conducts ceremonies such as the solstice ceremony.

Waiya also teaches schoolchildren about Chumash culture. And, he is working on creating a demonstration village. At the village, people will see how the Chumash once lived. Waiya is also working to protect Chumash cultural and historic sites.

Chief Pedro Yanonali

 # The Chumash Today

Today the Chumash live worldwide. Some live within their original lands. Many have become doctors, lawyers, and teachers. Now, about 5,000 people say they have Chumash ancestors.

Over the years, the Chumash lost a lot of land. Their homelands once covered about 7,000 square miles (18,130 sq km). Today, many Chumash groups have no land base. These Chumash are seeking lands, and they hope to become **federally recognized**.

The Santa Ynez Band of Chumash is the only federally recognized band of Chumash. Their reservation has only 128 acres (52 ha) of land, near Santa Barbara, California. They are trying to have more lands returned to them.

The Chumash still gather and hold ceremonies. The children are learning the stories and history of their people. The Chumash are working hard to protect their **culture** and environment, and to live in peace.

Grandfather Semu Huate, a Chumash medicine man

A chumash wearing
traditional clothing
at a powwow

Chumash girls wear
powwow dresses.
The Chumash
continue to hold
powwows year round
to celebrate their
culture.

A Chumash
man wears a
traditional
powwow
headdress.

Glossary

abalone - edible, spineless animals that cling to rocks.

cordage - ropes or cords made by twisting plant fibers.

cradleboard - a flat board used to hold a baby. It could be carried on the mother's back or hung from a tree so that the baby could see what was going on.

culture - the customs, arts, and tools of a nation or people at a certain time.

down - soft, fluffy feathers.

edible - able to be eaten safely.

estuary - the body of water where a river's current meets an ocean's tide.

federal recognition - the U.S. government's recognition of a tribe as being an independent nation. The tribe is eligible for funding and protection of its lands.

flicker - a spotted, North American woodpecker.

geometric - made up of straight lines, circles, and other simple shapes.

granary - a building used for storing grain.

harpoon - a spear made from wood or bone used to kill seals, walrus, and whales.

immunity - protection against disease.

kilt - a knee-length, skirt-like garment worn by men.

mission - a center or headquarters for religious work.

olivella - a beach animal with a shell and no backbone.

sinew - a band of tough fibers that joins a muscle to another part, such as a bone.

smallpox - a disease that can cause fever and skin irritations that leave blisters.

tiered - organized in such a way that some people are above others.

tule - a type of reed that grows in wetlands. Tule is native to California.

Web Sites

To learn more about the Chumash, visit ABDO Publishing Company on the World Wide Web at **www.abdopub.com**. Web sites about the Chumash are featured on our Book Links page. These links are routinely monitored and updated to provide the most current information available.

Index

iScience

Air and Weather:
Where'd My Hat Go?

by Emily Sohn and Judy Kentor Schmauss

Chief Content Consultant
Edward Rock
Associate Executive Director, National Science Teachers Association

NORWOOD HOUSE PRESS
Chicago, IL

Norwood House Press
PO Box 316598
Chicago, IL 60631

For information regarding Norwood House Press, please visit our website at
www.norwoodhousepress.com or call 866-565-2900.

Special thanks to: Amanda Jones, Amy Karasick, Alanna Mertens and Terrence Young, Jr.

Editors: Jessica McCulloch, Barbara Foster, and Diane Hinckley
Designer: Daniel M. Greene
Production Management: Victory Productions, Inc.

Library of Congress Cataloging-in-Publication Data

Sohn, Emily.

Air and weather : where'd my hat go? / by Emily Sohn and Judy Kentor Schmauss ;
chief content consultant, Edward Rock.
p. cm.—(iScience readers)

Summary: "Describes the importance of air and weather and the profound
effects they have on our daily lives. As readers use scientific inquiry to learn
about how and why air and weather are connected, an activity based on real
world situations challenges them to apply what they've learned in order to
solve a puzzle"—Provided by publisher.

Includes bibliographical references and indexes.

ISBN-13: 978-1-59953-403-9 (library edition: alk. paper)
ISBN-10: 1-59953-403-7 (library edition: alk. paper)

1. Air—Juvenile literature. 2. Atmosphere—Juvenile literature.
3. Weather—Juvenile literature. I. Schmauss, Judy Kentor. II. Rock, Edward. III. Title.

QC161.2.S66 2011
551.5—dc22
2011011433

Manufactured in the United States of America in North Mankato, Minnesota.

175N—072011

Contents

Note to Caregivers:

Throughout this book, many questions are posed to the reader. Some are open-ended and ask what the reader thinks. Discuss these questions with your child and guide him or her in thinking through the possible answers and outcomes. There are also questions posed which have a specific answer. Encourage your child to read through the text to determine the correct answer. Most importantly, encourage answers grounded in reality while also allowing imaginations to soar. Information to help support you as you share the book with your child is provided in the back in the **Additional Notes** section.

Words that are **bolded** are defined in the glossary in the back of the book.

Weather Report

Cloudy. Sunny. Rainy. Snowy. The **weather** might make you hot or cold, wet or dry. It affects what you wear and where you go. But how does the weather work?

In this book, you will learn about weather. You will also learn about air. After all, there would be no weather on Earth without air.

You will use what you learn to solve a mystery. It is the strange case of a missing hat!

Where Did Your Hat Go?

You put your hat on a park bench. Then you go play. It is windy out. When you come back for your hat, it's gone!

How can you find your hat?

Idea 1: Walk in a small circle. Then make your circle bigger and bigger. Soon, you will have searched the whole playground.

Idea 2: Find out which way the **wind** is blowing. Then follow the wind until you find your hat.

How can you tell by this picture that it is a windy day at the park?

Idea 3: Someone may have seen your hat or picked it up. Ask the other people at the park if they have seen it.

Which idea is best? Why?

Discover Activity

Finding the Wind

Materials
- bubble solution
- bubble wands

Sit quietly on the ground outside.

Can you feel any wind on your face?

Blow some bubbles.

Which way do the bubbles go?

What happens to your bubbles after you blow them?

Bubbles are more than just fun.
They can help you solve a mystery!

You can't see wind. But bubbles can show you where the wind is blowing.

Think back to the iScience Puzzle. How can blowing bubbles help you find your hat?

What Can You Do with Air?

You can't breathe underwater. But blowing underwater makes bubbles. They are made of air.

You breathe it in. You breathe it out. Air is all around you. Air is a **gas.**

Bubbles that come from a bottle are made of soap. When you make bubbles from a bottle with a wand, you fill soap with air.

How can you blow bubbles in water? Can you do this without getting wet?

The air you breathe can make things happen. For one thing, it can blow out candles on your birthday cake.

Making Air Move

Air can really move. And you can help it go.

One way to move air is to breathe in and out. You can also blow hard or soft. You can fill a balloon with air. And you can spin a pinwheel with it. You can use a fan to move it.

What else do you think can move air?

Air Movement

You cannot see wind. But flying leaves show you that the wind is blowing.

When air moves, it's called wind.

Your bubbles showed you what direction the wind was blowing.

Think about what wind can do outside on a gusty day. What other clues do you think you can use to "see" the wind?

On long trips, airplanes fly above the clouds. Why is the weather always clear above the clouds?

Did You Know?

Jet stream winds blow from west to east high in the sky. They can blow up to 200 miles (322 kilometers) an hour!

Jet streams help planes go faster when they fly eastward.

What would happen to your bubbles in a jet stream? What would happen to your hat?

When people want a big balloon to go up, they start a fire to heat the air inside. When they want the balloon to come down, they let the air cool.

The Heat Is On

Air can be hot or cold. As it gets warmer, it rises.

Try this. Make sure an adult is with you and says it's okay. Then, blow bubbles near a **radiator** or a heater.

What happens to the bubbles?

The Montgolfier brothers used hot air to fly in a big balloon. After that, others tried many balloon designs.

Connecting to History

The First Hot-Air Balloon

In 1782, two brothers attached a basket to a big bag. Their names were Joseph and Jacques Montgolfier.

They filled the bag with hot air. It flew!

This was the first hot-air balloon.

The Weather Outside

Clouds are part of the weather. What else is part of the weather?

Weather tells us what is happening in the air outside.

You can find out the **temperature.** This tells you if it's hot or cold.

Clouds can show how much water is in the air.

What else might clouds show?

Meteorologists

Meteorologists study weather. They are scientists. You can see them on your local news talking about the weather. They look into the future. They say if the Sun will shine when you wake up. They **predict** if it might rain this week.

These experts use many **tools.** Thermometers show how hot or cold it is. Rain gauges show how much rain has fallen.

Why would it help to know which way the wind is blowing?

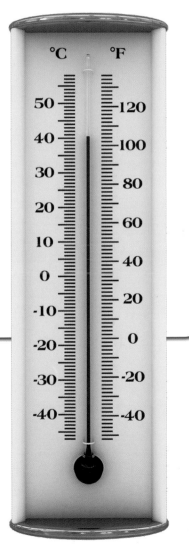

Knowing the temperature outside can help you decide what clothes to wear.

thermometer

16

Sunshine makes it fun to play outside. The Sun also plays a big role in all kinds of weather. Its heat warms the air, ground, and water in lakes, rivers, and oceans.

Then, tiny drops of water **evaporate.** That means the water changes from a liquid to a gas. And then it rises into the air.

With help from the Sun, water moves from the ground and the oceans up into the air. There, it makes clouds. What happens next?

Up high, the drops **condense.** That means they turn from a gas back into liquid water. The drops form around little specks of dust. This is how clouds form.

In the water cycle, water evaporates from the ocean (1) and from the land (2). Water condenses in clouds (3) and returns to the ground as rain or snow (4). Water can also seep into the ground (5). Then it moves into the clouds again. The cycle goes on.

Inside clouds, drops of water can get bigger. Then, water falls as rain or snow.

As it falls, water hits the ground and seeps into it. Water can eventually flow into streams, rivers, and even the oceans.

The Sun will shine again. And the **cycle** will keep going.

Clouds hold water in the air. But not all clouds are the same.

Cirrus clouds are high up and wispy.

| cirrus clouds | cumulus clouds | stratus clouds |

Different kinds of clouds bring us different kinds of weather.

Cumulus clouds are low and puffy. They look like cotton balls.

Stratus clouds are flat. They appear in layers.

Some kinds of clouds are more likely to bring storms.

What can the wind do to clouds?

Solve the iScience Puzzle

Where Did Your Hat Go?

Idea 1 is to walk in circles that get bigger and bigger. This way, you will search the whole park until you find your hat.

Idea 2 is to find out which way the wind is blowing. You could blow bubbles. Then, you could follow them until you find your hat.

Idea 3 is to ask other people if they have seen your hat.

Bubbles helped this boy get his hat back.

If there is a strong wind, idea 2 may work best. It would take you right to your hat. Idea 1 might take longer. But it might help you find your hat on a calmer day. Idea 3 could work. But it won't help you if no one has seen your hat.

Beyond the Puzzle

Now you have learned that air moves. And you used bubbles to tell which way the wind was blowing. You followed the wind to solve a mystery.

How else could you use wind? Read books or look online. Learn about wind power.

Then, design a machine that uses wind to do something. Draw the machine. Show how it uses wind to do work. There's a saying that if you know which way the wind blows, you are informed indeed!

How can looking at the sky tell you about the wind and the weather?

Glossary

cirrus: thin, wispy clouds high in the sky.

condense: change from a gas to a liquid.

cumulus: fluffy clouds that look thick.

cycle: something that happens over and over again in the same order.

evaporate: change from a liquid to a gas without boiling.

gas: something that is not a solid or a liquid.

jet stream: belt of fast-moving air high in the sky.

meteorologists: scientists who study the weather.

predict: to tell what you think will happen at some time in the future.

radiator: a metal box that heats a room when hot water or steam flows through it.

stratus: short clouds that form in layers.

temperature: a measure of the amount of heat.

tools: things to help with a job.

weather: a measure of the air, including how hot it is, how windy it is, and whether it is raining.

wind: moving air.

Further Reading

The Best Book of Weather, by Simon Adams. Kingfisher, 2008.

Air Is All Around You, by Franklyn M. Branley. Collins, 2006.

Wind and Air Pressure, by Alan Rogers and Angella Strelluk. Heinemann Educational Books, 2007.

Weather Wiz Kids, Wind. http://www.weatherwizkids.com/weather-wind.htm

University of Illinois Extension, Tree House Weather Kids. http://urbanext.illinois.edu/treehouse/

Additional Notes

The page references below provide answers to questions asked throughout the book. Questions whose answers will vary are not addressed.

Page 6: Caption question: The girl's hair is moving, so there must be wind.

Page 8: Blowing bubbles and watching where they move might show you in which direction something else, such as a hat, might be moving.

Page 9: You have to put your mouth in water and blow. You could do this without getting wet if you used a straw to blow the air into the water.

Page 12: Bubbles and a hat would probably move very fast in the jet stream.

Caption question: The weather is always clear above clouds because rain and other forms of precipitation come from clouds and move down to Earth, not up into the sky.

Page 13: Bubbles near a radiator or a heater float up.

Page 16: Wind direction can tell you whether storms in another place are heading your way.

Page 17: Caption question: The water comes back down.

Page 19: Wind can move clouds, or break them up, or push them together.

Index